POETRY with a PURPOSE

Stories, Ghosts, Truths

by JEROME DOLENZ

Poetry with a Purpose

by Jerome Dolenz

Poetry with a Purpose

© 2015 by Jerome Dolenz

Revised © 2018

All poems contained within these pages are the original creations of Jerome Dolenz. No reprinting, copying or any form of duplication is permitted without written consent of the author and publisher.

ISBN:
Paper 978-0-9961277-0-7
eBook: 978-0-9961277-1-4

Published by
Jerome Dolenz
Spicewood, Texas

Poetry with a Purpose

Dedication

To: Doris Dillon who was my grade school English teacher. Ms. Dillon did not give up on me or my classmates who struggled in her class. Through her strict discipline and no failure attitude, she lives in me today. She is a teacher's teacher! Doris Dillon's famous quote to each and every new class at the beginning of the year is ----- "I'm cranky and I mean to be!" I'm thankful and grateful you are a part of my life. Rest in peace.

11-17-1908 ---- 11-28-1995

Contents

Lonely Barn	8
Getting Old	10
Menger Hotel	12
Urbanite Cowboy	15
The Big Event	17
My Little Girl	19
All's Not Well	21
Mother	23
Cedar	25
Cemetery	27
Country Loving	29
Does Anyone Care	31
New Car	33
Opposites	35
Overalls	37
Paper Route	39
Red Head	42
Southern Men	44
Thank God	46

Poetry with a Purpose

Contents (Continued)

Tim	47
With Eaze	49
Wondering Eyes	51
In Times Again	53
Many Faces	54
My Beloved	56
Alcohol Slang	58
In Prayer	59
A Thought	61
The Machine	62
Stripes	63
Phony Hillary and Slick Willy	65
Trump	67
Commitment	70
Lotto	72
Lefty	74
Godspeed	76
Ted	78
Hats Off	81

Contents (Continued)

Done Right	84
Country Contrast	86
Stand By	88
About the Author	91

Lonely Barn

I use to have charm.
Are you interested in my history?
I'm whats left of the farm.
I'm feeling a little empty.

I'm, an old rickety barn standing out in the middle of a field.
There use to be a house, chicken coop and windmill.
I was the first to be built and have stood for many a year.
I was home to man, machinery and his critters.

I use to wear bright red with white trim.
Now, I'm pale gray, cracked and looking grim.
I haven't been painted with graffiti yet.
Too far from the city, I guess.

My walls have gaps. The wind and sun pass through.
Metal peeling off my roof. I'm leaning a little too.
I protect an old car worth more than me.
It still has most of it's paint, just a little dusty.

All of my stalls are empty now.
One can see chew marks from horses and cows.
Empty nail heads jut out from the walls.
Hung up were bridles, spurs and things overall.

The weather vane let's me know, she's up there still.
Now and then, with a gust of wind, she'll let out a little squeal.
One of my doors is off it's track.
I'm starting to look like an old shack.

As I stand here all alone, I think back on the good old days.
When the yard was busy with activities, my loft full of hay.
Rusty bailing wire hanging in the rafters.
Old dried manure on the floor.
There's a slight stench of a skunk from years before.

Jerome Dolenz

Corrals all gone. They plow right up to my door.
They may come to realize, I'm just an eyesore.
With a little pulling and bracing here and there.
A little oil, paint and some nails, I'd be square.

I stood up to what nature handed out.
I still have many good years, without a doubt.
One could easily scrap, bulldoze or burn me down.
Or, fix me up and keep me around.

Getting Old

Looking in the mirror.
Not getting any prettier.
Like an old boot.
Wrinkled, not cute.
I can be re-soled. - I'm seeing old.

Missing some teeth.
Don't get enough sleep.
Having this sagging.
Along with this cramping.
I'm moving slow. - I'm looking old.

Graying hair all around.
Seldom ever get to town.
No longer a flirty.
Go to bed early.
I'm going to fold. - I'm feeling old.

Have cuts and scrapes.
All kinds of pains and aches.
May look a little rough.
I'm still just as tough.
Like a billfold. - I've gotten old.

Hearing not too well.
Not even my smell.
Skin getting thinner.
All bruised up and tender.
Been told. - I know, I'm getting old.

Memory seems to fade.
Where's my maid?
Can't see very clear.
Where are you dear?
No need to scold - My mind old.

Jerome Dolenz

Plumbing in working order.
Some things a little shorter.
Taking the blue pill.
I can do it still.
I'm no centerfold. - I'm just old.

Age spots are coming.
All from too much sunning.
Feeling a little sicker.
Must be my ticker.
I need to be consoled. - I'm really old.

Getting a little dizzy.
Just part of my history.
Can't get enough air.
Now in a blank stare.
Heart starting to flutter.
Asking for my mother.
Lights starting to fade.
Slowly passing away.

He's stone cold. - All part of getting old.

Menger Hotel

Immigrants of German descent.
A small man with a big heart.
A boarding house was their intent.
His wife just as much a part.

In the middle of San Antone.
Across from the Alamo.
Stands a building of cut stone.
Once held Geronimo.

Emits antique smells.
Use to be a brewery.
Now it's a hotel.
With much history.

Many a notable have stayed.
Military, Hollywood, Presidents.
People played. Decisions were made.
Some are permanent residents.

Teddy Roosevelt frequented the bar.
He had a mission to fulfill.
Recruiting his rough riders from afar.
To march up San Juan hill.

Adina De Zavala spent years here.
Fasting three days at the shrine.
So the Alamo would not disappear.
Saving also the Spanish Governor's Palace in time.

J. W. Gates had his barbed wire show.
Just outside our corridor.
So that everyone would know.
In the hotel, place your orders.

Jerome Dolenz

Captain King has his suite.
Up on the second floor.
This is his retreat.
Enters his room without opening the door.

A frail little gal.
Reads a paper on a sofa chair.
Dressed Victorian style.
Seconds later, she's not there.

Outside your door at night.
One hears creaky sounds.
Is it Sally White?
Or security making its rounds?

With no one there.
Front lobby doors open.
There's certainly no air.
Spirits have spoken.

There were births and deaths.
We housed the wounded and sick.
From their first cry to their last breath.
Just part of our citizenship.

Through its tenure.
Three owners were to be.
Over 150 years of pleasure.
A feat throughout the century.

Scheduled to meet its demise.
A parking lot was to take its place.
Moody Foundation realized.
This would be a disgrace.

One will find superb cuisine.
Service is ideal.
Try their mango ice cream.
Enjoy your meal!

Poetry with a Purpose

Christmas and Halloween for our youthful.
Who would pitch this sale?
A tradition of helping people.
The amazing the Menger Hotel.

Photo courtesy of Ted Ernst Sarvata

Jerome Dolenz

Urbanite Cowboy

He dresses for the part, but he's no cowboy at heart.
To fulfill the role, you've got to have cowboy soul.

He's the average man.
Who wants a cowboy brand.
Wears ostrich boots.
But has no western roots.

He sports a big shiny buckle.
For us, thats a trophy medal.
He wants to learn the ropes.
Just to be like us folks.

Heavy starch on his pants.
Reckon he's got a chance?
Has a little less on his shirt.
He'll learn to curse.

Adjust your hat.
It's pert near on your back.
If you want to be that guy.
Say Howdy instead of Hi.

He drives a new truck.
With no scratches and such.
It'll get broke in.
If you go where we've been.

He drinks a little wine.
And all thats fine.
When you're out here.
You can't beat a cold beer.

He can dance the electric slide.
But he can't ride.
Ya, he sure does shine.
But, our world is dirt and grim.

Poetry with a Purpose

He dresses for show.
What we call rodeo.
Overcome our advantage.
Then, you'll be the complete package.

Jerome Dolenz

The Big Event

The rain stopped.
The sun came out.
Off came the top.
On to the route.

People lined the streets.
One last sharp turn.
Everything was complete.
No one concerned.

Agents stand down.
What's that about?
With no one around.
First shot rang out.

Body lurched forward.
Holding his throat.
Oh', dear Lord!
Is this a joke?

Seconds later head explodes.
Shot came from the right.
From the grassy knoll.
From witnesses on sight.

Motorcade sped away.
Agent now in tow.
Heading on the freeway.
The world put on hold.

Laying on a gurney.
The President, all but dead.
He envisioned our journey.
Remembering what he said.

Poetry with a Purpose

Can you hear the cadence of the drums?
Do you hear the clopping of the hoofs?
There lies a victim, succumbed!
Of America's deepest roots.

Jerome Dolenz

My Little Girl

After our two sons.
I wanted a little girl.
How about it Hun?
One with little curls.

The years went by.
With no success.
We ever so tried.
For a little princess.

It was quite late.
To our surprise.
Conception took place.
Twins, a girl and another guy.

Boy healthy as can be.
Little girl slow to arrive.
She has a disease.
Diagnosed as oxygen deprived.

Too weak to nurse.
Never cries, just sleeps.
It gets even worse.
She was born with four feet.

She has fight in her eyes.
Love her all we can.
Has a will to survive.
It's in God's hand.

She's daddy's little pet.
She almost died.
With no regrets.
We're happy she's alive.

Now, I have a daughter.
Just one last note.
I'm not the father.
She's our baby little goat.

Jerome Dolenz

All's Not Well

What have we become? A country out of control.
A nation parting from origin. God make us whole.

It starts in Washington D. C.
Those people work for us.
They put out their decrees.
Same people we no longer trust.

They receive all kinds of perks.
They vote to increase their pay.
For their quality of work.
How can they justify a raise?

Politicians are out of touch.
We fund their paycheck.
Don't try to manage us.
Lest you forget.

Half of them have law degrees.
Attended class on ethics.
It's wrong to deceive.
Why we are skeptics.

Giving you some guidance.
From the people who voted you in.
Review the Ten Commandments.
That's how you can begin.

To gain our respect.
Quit pandering to the special interests.
Abide the Constitution and protect.
Shun the Lobbyists.

Create a smaller government.
Pay off the debt.
Cut the budget.
Spend less.

Poetry with a Purpose

Keep our military strong.
Well equipped with good pay.
They will right the wrong.
Just stay out of their way.

Secure our borders.
Fairly market alternative fuel.
Restore law and order.
That's not being unreal.

Hold people accountable.
That includes you.
Set the example.
It's the right thing to do.

As one can tell.
Politician's not looking out for us.
We're mad as hell!
Step up or get off the bus.

In closing, create an environment.
Inviting the brightest to serve.
There's only discontent.
Not what our country deserves.

Jerome Dolenz

Mother

The greatest love. There is no other. It comes from above.
Through your loving mother.

There's nine of us kids.
She had no time for herself.
For all the things she did.
To unwind, she'd watch Lawrence Welk.

Mom had little if any formal wear.
No time or place to go.
For all of the kids she cared.
She just stayed home and watched her show.

Always trying to make ends meet.
Worried about next week's meals.
She would always manage to keep.
Our appetites fulfilled.

She was the last one to eat.
If, there was anything left.
She was quite petite.
What a beautiful brunette.

Never heard her complain.
Kept quiet and done her chores.
One could see she was strained.
She never swore.

She would wash our clothes.
Mend dresses and jeans.
Always at the cook stove.
Kept the house clean.

She would lend an ear.
Bandage, then kiss our hurts.
Taught us to persevere.
She was our comfort.

She would secretly cry at night.
Wondering what tomorrow would bring.
As soon as first light.
She was up, doing it all over again.

Mama never rested a day.
Always worrying about us.
That's always been her way.
She always made a fuss.

Thanks for taking the time.
For all the things you did.
For being so kind.
To all nine of your kids.

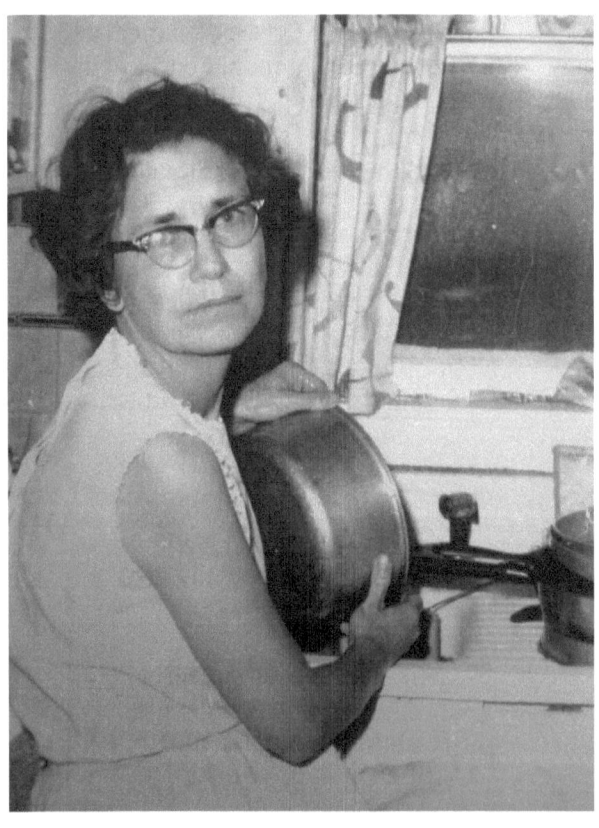

Jerome Dolenz

Cedar

The season we all fear.
Ash Juniper the tree to blame.
It comes every year.
Been cussed and called many a name.

An occurrence in this region.
All starts after the first freeze.
At it's worse, after the rainy season.
First sign is a simple sneeze.

Appears on the horizon as smoke.
The male tree pollinates the air.
Pardon me, may I clear my throat.
For some people, it can impair.

Contains an odor to ward off pests.
Moths shy away from clothes.
Good for linen closets and chests.
Have you any tissue? Got a runny nose.

My dog don't look so good.
Eyes watering and moping around.
Probably that darn old wood.
Won't load up and go to town.

Not easy to calculate.
Some symptoms hard to explain.
End up with a sinus headache.
Nasal passages constantly drain.

I could go on about remedies.
Everyone has their own.
What works for you, may not work for me.
Some people don't come out of their home.

Poetry with a Purpose

Come to Central Texas allergy free.
Settle in for a period of years.
Rest assured, one will catch the disease.
Also, causes itching in the ears.

Just Mother Nature in it's state.
One can measure the trade-off.
For three months, can you tolerate?
Did I hear someone cough?

Jerome Dolenz

Cemetery

One by one leaves fall from the trees.
Dancing all the way down.
Many more fall with a slight breeze.
Not many left, most on the ground.

I'm visiting graves today.
To recall the past.
Where my friends lay.
Who went too fast.

Gray clouds hang low.
Grass short and brown.
White crosses in rows.
No one else around.

Small American flags.
Their furls lay still.
They were young lads.
Wars have killed.

As I ponder the names and dates.
A lone bird in flight, blurts out a cry.
Appears to have lost it's mate.
As migration fills the sky.

Some tombstones have a picture.
And some have memento's.
One part of human nature.
For the world to see and know.

Fresh flowers on graves.
Most are dry and brittle.
Some scattered, which blew away.
Others artificial.

Sparsely visible tombs.
People of distinction.
Asleep in small rooms.
Their way of recognition.

Fresh dirt forms a mound wherein.
Over time, it will not stand out.
Like all the rest, who settled in.
The grass begins to sprout.

It brings to mind.
Right here I will lie.
It's just a matter of time.
Until we all eventually die.

Jerome Dolenz

Country Loving

City living not for me; country loving is what I need.

Buildings hiding the sun. People on the run.
You've got concrete, asphalt, traffic at a halt.
I've got dirt and gravel. A much easier travel.

You've got exhaust smells, all those hotels.
I've got a few motors, but only barnyard odors.
I've got fresh air. What you got there? - City living.......

You've got cops on every corner; trying to keep order.
Your streets not safe. You pull your shades.
Am I wrong? I don't have peeping toms.

You have leashes, bars, chains and other things.
Living for me, is not under lock and key.
I'll stick to my guns. I'm no townsman. City living.......

You have fashion stores and a whole lot more.
You have too many signs and too many fines.
I've got liberty, trees and no fees.

You live a fast pace. You're always late.
You have choice and noise.
I have calm, peace and no police. City living.......

You can keep your crowded schools.
With all their screwed up rules.
I'll take a small class. Where they still spank your ass.

You can keep your socialites.
We're not a like.
I'll take the farm over your charm. City living.......

All your friends are within.
I've got neighbors not strangers.
I'm not an urbanite. Sorry, you won't be my wife.

Poetry with a Purpose

Jerome Dolenz

Does Anyone Care

This old world is so corrupt. Doesn't anyone care anymore?
I know I've had enough. Or is it just me, that's so sore?

Whatever happen to customer service?
Lacking, once looked upon as good business. No one uses turn signals or shows courtesy; they just honk their horns and flip the birdie.
The law abiding people are few and far between, but the offenders are easily seen. Everyone's after the almighty dollar. People don't have time to say hi or even by; why bother?

The CEO demands a big salary.
They're happy paying little to the hourly.
What ever happened to equal justice?
If you have a lot of money you won't get busted.
Everyone coming across the border.
Don't mind the workers, but we need account and order.
The Politicians are not looking out for me;
They're taking care of friends and family.

No one stays married very long.
It's more than just a piece of paper and a wedding song.
Commitment is to give and take.
Why not do it for the children's sake?
Life is a test of how we treat people.
Nothing has changed, seems like it's gotten more evil.
One goes to church and what does one see?
Nothing, just empty pews staring back at me.

I'm trying to be straight and don't want to act like that.
I can't get use to these times.
Things are gloomy, where's the sunshine?
Will we ever return to the good old days?
When a man's word and handshake went a long way? For if I ever become one of them, please God send down one of your angels to rein me in.

Poetry with a Purpose

Jerome Dolenz

New Car

The old car has seen better days.
Way things are, it's on it's last leg.

Talking to the salesman, I changed my thoughts.
Looking for a trade in. Telling him it's tip top.

After much haggling, we settled on a price.
I took the beating. However, I'm driving something nice.

First thing to go. Those paper floor mats.
Make wonderful planes to throw. Cheap on their behalf!

Save that window sticker. Prolong those dealer plates.
Show off those features. Tags can wait.

Like the new car smell. Both hands on the wheel.
With all the whistles and bells, what a great feel!

I treat it like a lady at her bridal.
Or like a new baby, being cautious and gentle.

Driving too slow. What are you afraid of?
Not that it's old. It's like a new love.

Park from the main crowd. Don't want scratches or dings.
Just real proud. Hope to avoid the banging.

First few miles, respectfully use turn signals.
Being quite mobile. Only to become frugal.

Got my first blemish. I wasn't even there. Keyed, right
through the finish. Don't know why, when or where.

Time never healed. Thinking about the fact.
The way I feel, when I got that first scratch.

Not new anymore. Don't care where I park.
Dirt all over the floors. Lost that spark.

Ten years and thousands of miles;
time to do it all over again.
Excited about the new styles.
This time, I hope to negotiate and win!

Jerome Dolenz

Opposites

Don't lie, be honest.
With no reply, I promise.

It's hard to say good-bye.
Would never occurred, had I not said hi.

One has to wait, to begin.
Sometimes a mistake, not always a given.

Where's the love? Why the hate?
Comes from above. The other we create.

Half empty or half full?
Quite simply, both equal.

What's wrong? What's right?
The atomic bomb, that sits tight.

As young, as old.
I come, you go.

You're smart, not dumb.
Really aren't, what's your question?

Got started, can't stop.
Gets harder, may opt.

If one fails, blame only thee.
All hail, if you succeed.

If one makes a mistake, it may be correct.
If it's correct, it may be a mistake.

In birth and death, we part.
Both hurt, mother rest, journey starts.

Poetry with a Purpose

Jerome Dolenz

Overalls

I love my overalls. They come in pinstripe,
blue denim, white and brown if you recall.

There's Big Smith, Lee, Carhartt and Key. They come in
all sizes big and tall, even for the smallest of us all.
They are comfortable and fit just right, not too loose
and not too tight. You don't even need a belt. They even
have pockets to scratch yourself.

The men at the railroad wore them on the train.
They were the workers and engineers
dressed all the same.
They even have a hat with stripes to match.

Some folks like to wear their bibs high and some with
only one strap. Some like theirs around the waist when
they take a nap.
Some bottoms are rolled up and some are cuffed.
I like mine starched and straight, not like that other stuff.

The farmer wears his proud too.
In the summertime he wears no shirt, just his denim in
blue. When winter comes to be, he dresses in layers.
Rest assured overalls are on top for
everyone to see.

One can wear "new" bibs to church, with a white shirt.
They are easy to clean and show
little dirt. My friend was buried in his,
for that's all he owned. Lying there he looked
right at home.

The painter like their's white.
It broadcasts their colors and reflects the light.
It's free advertisement for their profession.
Have you ever seen a painter with no expression?

I've seen the ladies wear them.
They favor the shorts with red lace to attract us men.
They go real good without a blouse,
just draw up them straps and run about.

The construction men like their color too.
It's a blend of caterpillar, rusty iron and a
lineman's boot. They are rugged,
tough and last for years and will forgive too many beers.

The overall has come a long way.
Once they were called slops in their day. They
are making them slicker, with snaps, buttons,
patches and even zippers.
I love my overalls. They come in pinstripe,
blue denim, white and brown if you recall.

Jerome Dolenz

Paper Route

As a paper boy in a small town.
I met some interesting people.
Came to conclusion and found.
Most were nice, some were evil.

He greeted me with eleven cents in hand.
His tip was a penny.
He was a tall German man.
Townsfolk called him, "Big Ernie."

One of my customers, the Train Depot.
Built so close to the tracks.
A place that could be lethal.
Careful, I don't want a mishap.

Once dropped off a paper at the Gas Station.
Attendant said, I'll squeeze if you try to runaway.
Owner drives up. End of the situation.
Thank God! Pervert grabbed me where I'd rather not say.

Heading down a dirt road.
A part of the route I dread.
Rumor has it, as was told.
Man hung himself in that shed.

One of my customers, a well to do.
Thinks I run a free service.
Sorry to bring you the bad news.
Delinquent receipts show, you're worthless.

One day electricity went out on main street.
Further on towards the end of my route.
Man down, smoke coming out his feet.
Boom truck backed into the power line, no doubt.

Poetry with a Purpose

Another particular customer, I'll never forget.
I'll have to put it this way.
When it was time to collect.
She'd come to the door in a negligee.

Many years this dog barked and pulled at the fence.
For some reason he didn't like me.
One day he was quiet and absent.
Scared! Is he dead, or oh' mercy, free?

Always looked forward to Christmas.
Received mostly cards and food.
Some customers quite generous.
A few, never in the mood.

Worse part was monthly collection.
Some people wouldn't pay their dues.
Sometimes I would make an exception.
And sometimes, I would not deliver the news.

Newspaper company held a contest.
Most acquired new subscribers would win a bike.
If I won, my shoes would get a rest.
That machine fit me just right.

Now that I have a new bike.
I could cut my time in half.
I'd roll, then throw papers. Out of sight!
I lost a few customers over that.

Older, I started mowing yards.
I gave my route to my brother.
Telling him to keep up his guard.
I had an experience, like no other.

Jerome Dolenz

Red Head

I'm a red head; somewhere between a blond and a brunette.

We of Celt descent.
We favor red.
Known for being quite intimate.
That's the color of our head.

No need to bleach our hair.
That's what we value.
What we have is rare.
May I continue?

Our hair attracts attention.
We're not the shy type.
We clearly express our opinion.
We like a good fight.

Much farther on.
We never turn gray.
We turn into a sandy blond.
That's natures say.

Our skin being pale.
Freckles stand out.
We're quite well.
Have no doubt.

Don't get that golden tan.
We tolerate a little sun.
Hope you'll understand.
That's taught to everyone.

Can be somewhat temperamental.
We're set in our ways.
Also, known to be gentle.
Just part of our DNA.

Jerome Dolenz

We show our confidence.
How's our intellect?
There's assurance.
We're right there with the brunette.

History proves were leaders.
We're people of minority.
Just check the figures.
We have dignity.

We have no regrets.
With all being said.
We will make you a bet.
You'll be happy with red.

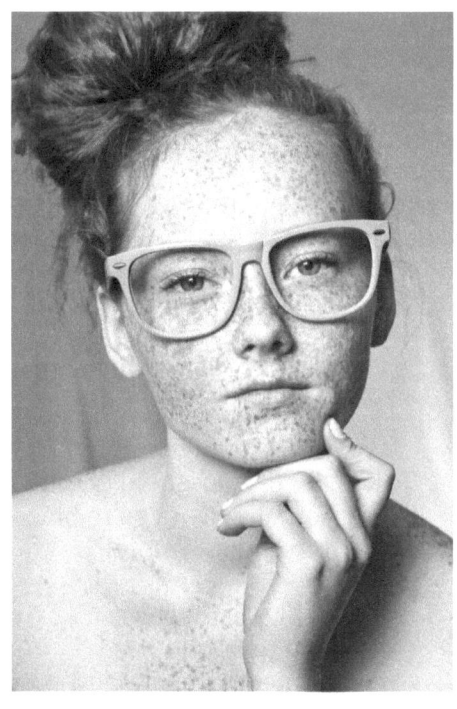

Southern Men

I'm just a southern man, schooled in Dixieland.
Brought up to please, a woman with needs.

Mama showed loving.
Daddy kept me true.
That's my upbringing.
It'll be good for you.

Got an accent.
Called southern drawl.
Comes from my environment.
Don't you know, y'all.

I may say "Darling", "Yes Please".
That's the way I talk.
You like sweet tea?
Take long walks?

I still tip my hat.
Open doors.
I'll watch your back.
I'm all yours.

I'll be your best friend.
You'll love my grits.
Like to fish and swim?
I've got some wits.

Work with my hands too.
Take care of household chores.
Cheer you up when you're blue.
I even have more.

I like barbecues.
Drinking cold beer.
Watermelon, honey-dew.
You're on my menu, dear.

Jerome Dolenz

I take my time.
Like to do it right.
Searching, I'll find.
Someone my type.

I like to shop around.
I'm not a one nightstand.
Looking until she's found.
Maybe you're my brand.

Like to live on a farm?
Roll around in the hay?
Want to see the barn?
How about it babe?

I'm a Christian man.
Not a fraud.
I'll take your hand.
If you believe in God.

Want to meet my mom?
Grandpa and Grandma too?
My daddy Tom?
And the rest of the brood?

Anyone out there?
Who would love this life?
Be willing to share.
And be their wife.

NEW
ORLEANS

Thank God

You sent your only Son to earth.
He's our savior that will set us free.
He was worshiped and scorned at birth.
Now he hangs from a tree.

Choose the road that's less traveled.
You have nothing to lose.
It's the path of the straight and narrow.
You are warned if you refuse.

You can believe or doubt.
The bible is selling well.
It's not hard to figure out.
You can go to heaven or go to hell.

Jerome Dolenz

Tim

One could tell he was special, right after birth.
He was so excited to be alive. Touched so many on this earth.
He was good to everyone. He genuinely cared about you.
Big smile with compassionate eyes was the first clue.
He was loved by so many. Don't know where to begin.
Many descriptives to fulfill. Welcome our Brother Tim.

When he stepped into a room, most heads would turn.
Everyone consumed. Who's this mid-westerner?
Always made time to honor your request.
He sacrificed himself to bring out your best.
No doubt he was a perfect ten.
How does one rate such a man? Our Brother Tim.

School days - His physique was short and thin.
In between classes, pranksters waited for him.
They hung him by his waist belt on a closet hook.
Only to return before the bell, so he could get his books.
They were perturbed! He just returned the favor with a grin.
Not many could take that! Other than, our Brother Tim.

Flying was his passion. He started out with a kite.
Kids felt welcomed. Come to watch. He was so polite.
Received his wings. Progressed over the years.
Became a test pilot. Respected by his peers.
On a minutes notice he would be in the air once again.
One such call by Mother for a leaky repairman.
Our Brother Tim.

Known to never turn anyone down.
Fed-Ex friend just happened to be around.
Want to go up for a quick flight?
Just a minute, I'll clear it with my wife.
Plane went down. Never to be seen again.
Both had same first names; our Brother Tim and his friend.

Poetry with a Purpose

Jerome Dolenz

With Eaze

Still waters on a pond.
Casts an image looked upon.
Slight breeze.
Image leaves.
Got a fish on.

Flowers scattered all about.
Heads all seeded out.
First freeze.
Drops seeds.
Ready for a new sprout.

Allergy season here again.
Pollen teamed up with the wind.
Nasty sneeze.
Excuse me!
Not a good blend.

I've smoked all my life.
Ignored the doctor's warning, right.
Whistling wheeze.
Can't breathe.
Have you a light?

Met her in the pool hall.
Far from being a doll.
Real sleaze.
Check please.
Better luck in the mall.

To remain in the hunt.
Baseballs desperation bunt.
"The Squeeze".
With ease.
Now were out in front.

Eyebrows in need of repair.
Using precise care.
Quick tweeze.
Fits me.
Gets rid of unwanted hair.

An appropriate clause.
If, one has probable cause.
Search seize.
Warrant please.
One of our many laws.

Jerome Dolenz

Wondering Eyes

Her
Use to open the door.
We would take our walks.
Buy me roses and more.
Have our talks.
I can't deny. – My wondering eyes.

Him

Always at the store.
Never have money.
Always feeling poor.
Use to call me honey.
I can justify. – My wondering eyes.

Use to say I'm cute.
Always seem annoyed.
Always in dispute.
I've lost all my joy.
I'm not surprised. - I have wondering eyes.

Can't fit in your swimsuit.
Won't let me have any toys.
Always in pursuit.
Don't let me go out with the boys.
Likewise. – Guys have wondering eyes.

Always out of town.
Always working late.
With no one around.
We don't communicate.
Never satisfied. – Can't hide wondering eyes.

Screening my calls.
Checking my receipts.
Don't trust me at all.
Saying I'm a cheat.
I don't womanize. – Despite wondering eyes.

Poetry with a Purpose

Her
Always watch sports.
Keep your nose in a book.
I never get support.
You can't even cook.
I despise. – Your wondering eyes.

Him
Dresses too short.
Too many shoes.
Thats my report.
Always an issue.
You criticize. – With wondering eyes.

Don't go to church.
Never visits my folks.
Always complain of work.
This is not a joke.
That's my reply. –Wondering eyes.

Let's meet halfway.
Make no mistake.
Let's not stray.
For the children's sake.
Can we compromise? – Our wondering eyes.

Let's give it a try.
I'll do my part.
Can you comply?
Comes from the heart.
Let's sacrifice. – No wondering eyes.

May I have the last say?
For those of you in trouble.
Doesn't have to be this way.
Please remain a couple.
No good-byes. – No wondering eyes.

Jerome Dolenz

In Times Again

Born with bare gums. - Old and back to the original ones.

Young always fussing. - Old just the same, but cussing.

Born with little hair. - Old and just as bare.

Young and potty trained. - Old with a diaper again.

Born with underdeveloped brain. - Old mind becoming the same.

Young receive soft food. - Old people crave it too.

Born with baby fat. - Old and it all comes back.

Babies require attention. - Elderly require supervision.

Babies have caps and blankets. - Elderly have hats and jackets.

Babies have a distinct smell. - Elderly as well.

Babies take naps. - Elderlies habitat.

Babies have strollers. - Elderly have chauffeurs.

Babies lack muscle. - Elderly are feeble.

Babies, all that we are. - Elderly, its based on my memoir.

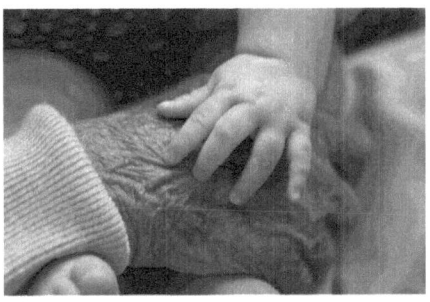

Many Faces

A lost look on the face.
Not blinking, just a stare.
Lacking memory, faintly a trace.
Looking into the empty space.
Eyes searching, but nothing there.
Slowly rocking in the chair.

Old sagging bags under the eyes.
Watering and bloodshot, an off-white.
The baldness one can't hide.
Not enough hair to comb to the side.
Appears content and jovial despite.
Arguing for years in courtroom fights.

Right side of the face droops down.
Talks out the corner of the mouth.
Mixed mumble, the only sound.
Hard to smile, mostly a frown.
Gets frustrated, wants to shout.
After the stroke, everything went south.

Big smile shows pronounced gums.
Pinkish color, sign of healthy teeth.
Top incisors, being the longest ones.
Slight tease with the tip of the tongue.
Smeared lipstick an added treat.
Go ahead, please speak.

No visible ears, only holes.
Eyelids, eyebrows and head lacking hair.
Missing cartilage at the nose.
Lips pulled back, teeth always show.
Scarred mismatched skin, burns everywhere.
Inevitably, people can't help but stare.
They, remain calm and composed.
Just thank them for their service in warfare.

Jerome Dolenz

My Beloved

A Cinderella story in its making.
I was introduced to her by a friend.
As our eyes met, there came a bonding.
She has long black hair, with a frosted blend.
Beauty on the outside and well within.
No doubt, she's muy bonita.
Gifted with kindness and care, a Godsend.
An Angel from Heaven, mi Chica.
She's my beautiful West Texan.
My sweet little Senorita.
My gorgeous little Mexican.
My wonderful wife Lupita.

Despite all the things I do.
She's always been there, a given.
What you did for me, will come back to you.
It has been said and also written.
Love is not blind, nor is it hidden.
It's high time, I pay back my Senora.
I'm giving you a sample of Heaven.
It will be, our little fiesta.

She takes an interest in my hobbies.
Involving herself, that's my woman.
Secretly though, she would rather make tamales.
She's sweet like a peach, rarely a lemon.
Spiritually, she's a God loving person.
She remains close to the Blessed Lady Madonna.
Not surprised, her Saintly name is Guadalupe The Virgin.
Our lives are enriched by our faith. Viva Maria.

Jerome Dolenz

Oh, how the years have gone by.
Let us tell you all about our living.
After thirty eight years, were still unified.
Blessed with babies, both are young gentlemen.
Neither one married, grandkids we're not missing.
Both reside at our hacienda.
Not much to say, other than.
Both love mamma's salsa and tortilla's.
She's my beautiful West Texan.
My sweet little Senorita.
My gorgeous little Mexican.
My wonderful wife Lupita.

Alcohol Slang

Alcohol has many names, starting with **Adult Beverage**.
Distilled outside and in seclusion, that's **Moonshine**.
Once used as a cure-all, the **Hot Toddy**.
Served with meals and special occasions that's **Wine**.
On a hot day one would want a **Cold One**.
People who drink draft beer, call it **Suds**.
Some go as far as ordering whats called a **Shotgun**.
Or, you may call for a regular old **Bud**.
Some people entertain with a little **Brandy**.
And some refrain, suggesting serving **BYOB**.
Of course on New Years, out comes the **Bubbly**.
Some like an olive in their **G And T**.
Some people prefer the **Hard Stuff**.
It's what most folks call **Whiskey**.
To some it's known as **Rot Gut**.
I prefer sticking with my **Brew-ski's.**
More independents are making their own **Brew**.
A known company uses spring water, **Colorado Kool-Aid**.
One can take a tour and sample **A Few**.
Pop the top, it bubbles up like **Champagne**.
There's a certain type of **Booze**.
Some folks call it **Juice**.
It's **Fire Water**, also known as **Mountain Dew**.
It's even been called **Hooch**.
No, I'm not an **Alky**.
Not even a **Boozer**.
Sometimes I get a little **Tipsy**.
Not enough to be called a **Juicer**.
I'm far from a **Drunkard**.
Sometimes I may get a little **Pickled**.
But, I never ever get **Plastered**.
Don't get labeled.
Drink, be responsible.

Jerome Dolenz

In Prayer

As I soaked in the tub praying the rosary.
A thought occurred in my mind.
I should write my own eulogy.
No disrespect, but it comes at the wrong time.

I should have been concentrating on God.
That's always been hard to do.
I find it quite odd.
My rosary keeps breaking in two.

Hopefully, that's not a bad omen.
Using needle nose pliers to fix it up.
It's weak, old and always broken.
Moreover, I keep clamping the links shut.

One evening halfway through prayers.
My rosary again split in two.
Interruption and tired of the repairs.
I'm thinking, what shall I do?

For starters, stay focused and don't daydream.
After properly burying the other.
Out of many, I chose a rosary of green.
It's special, it was my wife's mother's.

Praying, I'm trying to stay focused on God.
As my fingers run along the beads.
I think it's rather odd.
I would think about my eulogy.

Besides, I'm undressed and wet.
I don't have pen or paper at hand.
Actually, that's something I'd like to forget.
I just want to be remembered as the rosary repairman.

Poetry with a Purpose

Jerome Dolenz

A Thought

What and when was the first picture?
With deep thought, answer goes to God.
If, one believes in Bible scripture.
His vision was quite broad.
Started with an image of earth.
But, I find it rather odd.
That some people would assert.
That my thinking is flawed.
Don't profess to be an expert.
However, film needs light for exposure.
In the beginning it was dark and void, a factor.

Then came along man.
With humans leaving their mark.
Restless minds to ever expand.
It begins deep within the heart.
Everyone possesses a talent.
So, please come out of the dark.
Expose your gifts, don't be silent.
Be it photography, literature or the arts.
All of us are special and different.
One can see where pictures began.
Started with God and ended up with man.

The Machine

I've dreaded this day.
It's been a long wait.
It brings one to pray.
That everything will be OK.
It will determine one's fate.

As I walk through the doors.
Faces slowly turn, showing despair.
Some reading, some ignore.
I'm joining them, to be explored.
Something we all share.

Seeking to find the unknown.
Be lying, if not scared.
All that's being shown.
Everyone in their zone.
People can't help but stare.

One by one names are called.
People led to rooms to seek the truth.
Anticipation and worrisome worst of all.
Being one's relief or downfall.
Pictures become one's proof.

My turn to be screened.
Zapping with accuracy, it doesn't lie.
Will it find me dirty or clean?
After all, it's just a machine.
Not fun, going through an MRI.

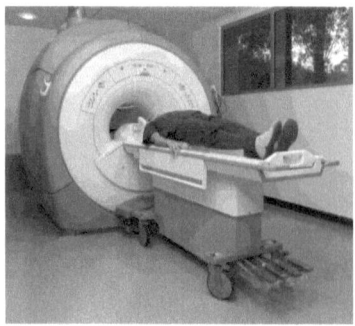

Jerome Dolenz

Stripes

Many objects display a pattern.
Some are dull and some incite.
Some old and some modern.
The one I'm about to write.
Comes from symbols of stripes.

Foremost, the American flag.
Thirteen lines representing colonies.
Occasional, it does sag.
Only to come back, waving honorably.
The stars and stripes bear many stories.

Men and women of America's best.
Rank reflects the number of stripes.
Medals decorate their chest.
Hash marks signify the number of fights.
Soldiers deserve respect, be polite.

A referee controls the game.
Dressed in black and white.
Fans disagree and players complain.
All one can do is gripe.
To the one who wears the stripes.

Dressed to standout.
They wear a suit of pinstripe.
There's certainly no doubt.
They're not your average type.
Convicts are easy to sight.

Utilized as camouflage.
Animals have their stripes.
To improve the odds.
For tigers and snakes alike.
Or to avoid the bite.

Poetry with a Purpose

Barbers display their distinct sign.
A revolving cylinder type.
A part of their lifeline.
Stripes of blue, red and white.
Some even have a light.

To signify power and speed.
Muscle cars display racing stripes.
Decal or painted on the body.
From the hood to the tailpipe.
Car manufactures exploit the hype.

Candy cane peppermint stick.
How many licks, before you bite?
Don't know, but I want to quit.
My last verse to write.
Have I left out any stripes?

Jerome Dolenz

Phony Hillary and Slick Willy

It was called Travel-Gate. Hillary allegedly fired
government employees. For her own interests, at any
rate. Only to re-hire Clinton cronies. I'm just getting
started, I've only begun. Hillary, what have you done?

Then came White-Water. The Clinton's, associates of an
alleged crime. Fed's shut down the account, reveals the
blotter. The McDougal's guilty, did jail time. Clearly a
scam was being run. Hillary, what have you done?

Next is File-Gate.
FBI background files, improperly obtained.
Also, files removed from Vince Foster's office estate.
And Hillary's law firm records missing, never explained.
After all this, the Foster's lose their loved one.
Hillary, what have you done?

White House becomes a fund-raiser for Clinton.
So enticing, a good opportune for the Mrs.
800 plus supporters, rented out the bedroom of Lincoln.
She is also eyeballing the art, furniture and dishes.
The Clinton's allegedly pillaged, many items stolen.
Hillary, what have you done?

Hillary's husband was impeached.
For obstruction of justice and lying.
"A vast Right-Wing conspiracy," Hillary preached.
Gennifer Flowers, Paula Jones and others, all identifying.
Covering your husband's behavior, wrong and dumb.
Hillary, what have you done?

Poetry with a Purpose

Then there was the Pardon-Gate guy.
Political contributions for the tax evasive Mark Rich.
Let's not forget the Bosnia airport sniper lie.
Nothing new, her same old pitch.
Is deceiving, really all that fun?
Hillary, what have you done?

Then came the fateful Benghazi Disaster.
"What difference at this point, does it make?"
A video provoked fighting, false and shame on the media.
Secretary Clinton's thoughtlessness, created much heartache.
The difference is, wives lost husbands, mother's lost sons.
Hillary, what have you done?

Last, but not least of them all.
The E-mail Scandals and the Clinton Foundation.
E-mailing is a "convenience" Hillary explained, say windfall.
All for the love of money, from questionable contributions.
You're not above the law, is this treason?
Hillary, what have you done?

One is known by the company you keep.
You reap what you sow.
Do we all want a repeat,
of the Obama and Hillary show?
America, before you vote, ask yourself this question.
Hillary what have you done?

Jerome Dolenz

Trump

Coming down the escalator with his wife.
Knowingly, his odds look dim.
Why am I doing this? I have a great life.
Because I love America, its sink or swim.
President Trump speaks the truth from the heart.
Honesty, upsets the media, the left and some on the right.
They all tried to take him down. Trump is too smart.

One can judge a man by observing his children.
Well schooled and disciplined is Don Jr., Ivanka and Eric.
Warming up in the ranks is Tiffany and Barron.
Wife Melania, fluent in 5 languages, native being Slavic.
President Trump sacrifices his time, family and money.
All for America, his mission.
A precedence is set, a first in history.

It all started with his hair, real or fake?
Then came the question of Trump's net worth.
It was all about nothing, their mistake.
No apology, what else can they unearth?
Then came 16 candidates, all taking their turns.
One by one, all withdrew after the debates.
Trump remained center stage and rightfully earned.

Commanding media attention, with his appeal.
Unlike his opponent, who spent millions.
It's all in his book, "The Art Of The Deal."
Federal Reserve prints more paper, U.S. debt in the trillions.
He will rid waste, cut the budget and spend less.
He's created jobs and called for Obama Care repeal.
Our Country is safe, strong and great again, yes!

Businesses' considering leaving America, think twice.
It's not patriotic, it will hurt your bottom line.
Your actions will be countered, with a 35% tax, nice!
He's trimmed excess regulation and corporate taxes, a good sign.
To encourage small businesses' and invigorate the economy.
Trump revised the estate tax, protecting ones' rights.
Also, defending the Constitution and upholding our laws fully.

Trump has strengthened our Military and attends to our Vet's.
He protects sensitive documents and restored foreign relations.
Holding people accountable, that incite terroristic threats.
He has required our Allies, to fulfill their obligations.
He's building the wall and issuing "merit" permits.
Securing our border and humanely reviewing who's left.
All for the stoppage of drugs, thugs and misfits.

Trump does not support political correctness.
Discouraging Common Core while offering Charter Schools.
Resurrecting the words God, prayer, and Oh, Merry Christmas.
If a political party controls our speech, we are fools.
Improving our bridges, airports, highways and the inner city.
He's a builder that creates jobs and promotes good business.
Endorsed by: NRA, Police, Border Patrol and the Military.

Trump has surrounded himself with competent people.
He has appointed judges with the likeness of Scalia.
Unifying the Country once again, making it civil.
He speaks the truth, unlike the Fake Media.
President Trump is not for sale in Washington D.C.
He's not a Politician, he's a Patriotic Rebel.
He fights for the common worker and retirees'.

A vile Justice Department, the Underground.
Besmirched our President, who endured threats, lies and leaks.
They didn't want him around.
Fighting with facts, have you enjoyed the Presidents' tweets?
Trump soars like the American eagle.
Free, keeping his eyes on the corrupt Elites.
He shows compassion and protects the American people.

Jerome Dolenz

The survival of our Republic was in jeopardy.
President Trump defeated a soft Coup.
Fending off evil and saving our Liberty.
America owes President Trump, a lasting thank you.
Most in their "right" minds would concur.
Trumps' perception and leadership is wholeheartedly.
He has earned a placement of Honor.

The sacred monument Mount Rushmore.
With Washington, Jefferson, Theodore Roosevelt and Lincoln.
Their attributes are worth fighting for.
President Trump carried the torch in their vision.
Trump duly belongs with the 4 Presidents overhead.
He "Made America Great Again", our Republic Savior.
"Knowing your toil is not in vain," as Scripture read.
God willingly, and with Americas' help, let's embed
President Trump, after all that's been said.

Commitment

After completing my lap swim.
I'll straddle the aqua bike.
While listening to country hymns.
I'll pedal to my delight.
Stopping only, after the third song.
All promises be kept, right!

Been pedaling all along.
Legs weary from swimming.
Two country hits are now gone.
However, I'm still pedaling.
Due to a commercial break.
I recall my oath undertaking.

After the third song, I'll forsake.
Airing, is weather and traffic reports.
My legs are starting to ache.
Come on, let's keep it short.
Now, promoting a weight loss trend.
Next, their talking about sports.

When will this ever end?
Restraining me causes resentment.
DJ please be my friend.
I'm honoring a commitment.
Please play just one more tune.
Your commercials are relentless.

Not committing again, anytime soon.
I want to be done, through.
Shortly it will be noon.
I was feeling the blues.
Garth Brooks saves the day.
He came on after the news.

Jerome Dolenz

Singing, "Two Pina Coladas," yea.
Honoring a contract, is self pride.
How many of you would convey?
All unfilled commitments, died.
Pledges large or small, claim!
To commit, says that one tried.

If one reneges, you're the blame.
You're as good as dirt.
So keep a good name.
Pedaling, as it did hurt.
Finished, my conscience is clear.
Hold on until the end, exert!

Lotto

People all over the world.
Struggle to fulfill their means.
Many fantasize of being rich.
In their wildest dreams.
A few experience reality.
Most get that itch.
To play the lottery.

The luck of the draw.
If, I select all six numbers.
Then all would be well.
This could lead to answers.
To bring me out of debt.
Or, the road to hell.
A windfall, some regret.

Ethical work is relevant here.
Refusing the option of "quick pick."
By methodically selecting numbers.
I'm willing to work for it.
Wanting to earn my pay.
Calculators can do wonders.
Let's go make some hay.

Start with a positive outlook.
Numbers frequently drawn, choose.
Or, make selections at random.
Mark what works for you.
One could use birthdays or ages.
Merely aiming to beat the system.
All to increase ones' wages.

Jerome Dolenz

Prayers are finally answered.
Still can't believe I won.
Will I take the annual payment?
Shall I take the lump sum?
I beat the odds by believing.
After all, I'm the claimant.
If only, I wasn't dreaming.

Lefty

A myth from the old world.
Stigmatized, cursed and shunned.
More prevalent in boys than girls.
I'm referring to the left-handed ones.
They tried to change us, the grandparents, teachers and nuns.
Why does everyone make such a fuss?
We're not sinister, clumsy or dumb.
We've got the right stuff.
Being creative, we've learned to adjust.
We certainly have been branded.
We come from a different class.
We can cope and even multi-task.
All because, we're left-handed.

The right-handed ones, who sit left of a south-paw.
Neither gets along, with round tables.
Not enough room to feed their jaws.
They tend to rub elbows.
Lefties' favor the square ones, the corners enable.
Good luck in college, finding a desk.
It's just one more hurdle.
Contorting your body, you've passed the test.
Be nice, if they would all swivel.
How about a little respect?
The only thing "right" so far,
the steering wheel location, on the American car.
Thank you Ford, for being the architect.

Jerome Dolenz

Michelangelo, Beethoven, Mozart,
Henry Ford, Da Vinci, Einstein,
Mark Twain, Churchill, Joan of Arc,
All, in their right minds.
All are lefties, all one of a kind.
If it's not right, then go left.
We're easy to spot, and easy to find.
In comparison, a blond is to a brunette.
It's only in the color, what the heck?
We draw attention, everyone is surprised.
We're just being ourselves.
Just like everyone else.
Not a big deal, but it shows in ones' eyes.

Handles on the wrong side.
Rod and reel turned downward, weird.
Spiral notebooks and us collide.
Letters on the chalkboard disappear.
As the hand moves directly and smears.
We're easy to spot, we leave a sign.
We pay a premium for our gear.
Our check-mark is easily defined.
After all this, we seldom whine.
With all the traits, that we possess.
In extreme cases, we utilize the right hand.
Only in emergencies, because we can.
We've all been blessed.
The right, along with the left.

Godspeed

A young Priest arrives from Colombia.
His greetings are sincere and true.
And Oh my, that charisma.
The things he can make us do.
He comes to serve me and you.

Father, thank you for listening to our woes.
Working tirelessly to satisfy.
Advising the young, comforting the old.
From baptisms, to friends who died.
You've enriched so many lives.

When a circumstance arises.
You, remain focused and cool.
Some of us get excited.
As a general rule.
Always turns out, to be minuscule.

Having vision for our Parish.
With a mindset of ---- "can do."
Events, we will always cherish.
You brought out our best, we grew.
You left a standard, to live up to.

Father Jario, you've come a long way.
Adjusting well to our culture.
How does one convey?
Your orders, at this juncture.
Biblical speaking from 2nd Timothy of scripture.

"For I am now ready to be offered
and my time of departure
is at hand."

Father Jario, you will never, ever truly part.
You left your legacy and it's fitting.
You will always be remembered, through your art.
I was just thinking.
It's the end, of the beginning.

Ted

As I shake her hand.
It feels like cracked leather.
I swear it's a Man.
If I didn't know better.
Is she female?
I'm afraid to ask.
If one can't tell.
Best let it pass.

She can ride with the best.
She takes no guff.
A man of the west.
She's wild and tough.
Her name is Ted.
Stay on her good side.
It's been said.
She's all eyes.

She points out mistakes.
She's direct and sure.
For ones' own sake.
Better agree with her.
This gal called Teddy.
No lovable bear.
She's cold and testy.
Not your average mare.

She don't own a dress.
No time for romance.
Then one might guess.
She don't like to dance.
She'd rather tend cattle.
Than take a whirl.
I'm somewhat rattled.
Boy, is this a girl?

Jerome Dolenz

Then there's dumb.
Once was called mister.
She belted that one.
It's ma'am not sir!
Later, seeing her grin.
Saying, I've had enough.
Of them their men.
It's time to go, giddy-up.

Cow punching takes a toll.
Reckon it's the end.
No more post holes.
Or riding the pens.
Done sold her horse.
Bought an RV park.
Nature runs its course.
Another cowhand parts.

The one who cared.
Stubborn in her ways.
That's Teddy St. Clair.
This is her say.
Better to do something.
And do it right.
Rather than do nothing.
You have not tried.

I like a cowgirl.
That's saddle sore.
Been kicked a time or two.
Doing cowboy chores.
Partakes in chew.
Just don't call her senor.

Poetry with a Purpose

Jerome Dolenz

Hats Off

I'm known as the "boss" of the plains.
A simple crown, with an average brim.
With Mexican influence, Stetson my name.
Custom sizes for her and him.
I'm like the sombrero, but smaller compact.
Resistol, Bailey, all the others came.
I'm just a cowboy hat.

Steamed and shaped to fit one's style.
From the average Joe, to the high bred.
Some dented, creased, rolled up, plum wild.
Defines character, it's been said.
They want my look and feel to be exact.
I'm part of their heritage, one's profile.
I'm just a cowboy hat.

So I see, I've caught your eye.
With an assortment of colors and mementos.
Some, cock me to the side.
Sporting a favorite feather or logo.
In addition, to being attractive to look at.
I have many functions, that I provide.
I'm just a cowboy hat.

I've hauled water, fed out grain.
Gathered eggs, fanned campfires.
Protecting heads, from sun, snow, wind, rain.
I'm slowly lowered to honor, pray, admire.
Time to pull down for a nap.
I'm all about soothing one's brain.
I'm just a cowboy hat.

Seldom do I part, I need some air.
Occasionally, let me and thy head breathe.
I can see why, you don't have any hair.
Your scalp is lacking, vitamin D.
On second thought, I take it back.
Unrecognizable, folks may stare.
I'm just a cowboy hat.

Like men, women wear my signature too.
Some traditional and some sophisticated.
Sporting colors of black, white, red, blue.
Having vision, look what she's created.
A fancy headdress, with matching chaps.
All for show and lassoing cowboys like you.
I'm just a cowgirl hat.

I'm forced over the ears, anticipating a hard ride.
One last slap, to the top of my crown.
I'm all set, he's satisfied.
We wreck, he's OK, I'm stomped into the ground.
Manured soiled, inside out, after all that.
I'm dusted off, pushed out, once again I survived.
I'm just a cowboy hat.

With 100 degree days, a wind so little.
Salt stains protrude, like snowy peaks.
Now, I'm hard and brittle.
There's a smell, a smell that reeks.
One can read me like a topical map.
There's mountains, plateaus, valleys, and water that stinks.
I'm just a cowboy hat.

Jerome Dolenz

One final task before I go.
When they lay my friend to rest.
Just promise me and tell me so.
Undertaker, place me upon my master's chest.
Crown down, please don't lay me flat.
So all can see my small memorial bow.
I'm just a Cowboy hat.
For all the Cowboys and Girls who preceded, God bless their souls. Hats Off!

Done Right

Whatever task, one takes upon.
Do it half-ass, you don't belong.
Pay close attention, listen up y'all.
In sweeping a floor or teaching a class.
Clean behind the door, opt to fail or pass.
Do it right or don't do it at all.

In representing oneself, be aware of your faults.
Like everyone else, people tend to talk.
Keep an open mind, never create a wall.
If one is going to lead, position oneself in front.
In order to succeed, never become distant.
Do it right or don't do it at all.

Monitor ones' actions, it's either wrong or precise.
Always use caution, think twice.
Whatever it be, big or small.
Trust your gut, act upon feelings.
Use the word but, point out shortcomings.
Do it right or don't do it at all.

Surround oneself with competent people.
Ask for help, find someone truthful.
No one likes recalls.
Don't be taken for a fool.
There's an area of gray, not taught in school.
Do it right or don't do it at all.

In making decisions, the wise consult.
Ask a lot lot of questions, then pray and hope.
When it comes to downright, it's your call.
Potentially could bring, life or death.
A clean conscience always rests.
Do it right or don't do it at all.

Jerome Dolenz

Just think, about a munitions worker.
In a blink, it could be all over.
A difference of, a hurricane or squall.
Mistake by a barber, a forgiven act.
Not a goner, the hair grows back.
Do it right or don't do it at all.

Put people first, before the dollar.
It's well versed, take it from this Author.
Being lax, one takes the fall.
Follow this guide, gain the respect.
This ain't no lie, it's what people expect.
Do it right or don't do it at all.

Country Contrast

That ain't country.
Pick another name.
Just call it something.
It ain't the same.

The lyrics you sing.
And the rhythm you play.
Doesn't have that ring.
That in no way.
Is western swing.
What's ailing you?
Is a steel guitar.
A fiddle or two.
Define who you are.
Who's fooling who?

If you're confused.
It's not rock and roll.
Short of the blues.
Damn shore not soul.
It's catch twenty two.
Identify your brand.
It's just a trend.
It's not big band.
Nor gospel, amen.
On the other hand.

What to call it.
Don't have a clue.
Not a country hit.
It's music of new.
You must admit.
There is a Hank.
A Jimmy Rodgers.
You broke rank.
They deserve honor.
And I'll be frank.

Jerome Dolenz

Nashville, is king of Pop.
Don't mess with Texans.
Where country music rocks.
If you want direction.
Just go to Luckenbach.
What you lack?
Is traditional values.
Country coming back.
I'm a telling you.
And that's my rap.

That ain't country.
Pick another name.
Just call it something.
Because, it ain't the same.

Stand By

The NFL has rules.
It's as simple as that.
Why do you ridicule?
Abide by the fact.
No leadership, no Ump.
It's not fair or cool.
To disrespect President Trump.

If one is to take a stand.
Why lower yourself to kneel?
You're pissing on the fans.
Yes, it's a big deal.
Sport fans have "shrunk".
I hope you understand.
It's not because of Trump.

Pittsburgh pick another mascot.
United Iron workers take a stand.
Save your hard earned money, boycott.
Steel workers do give a damn.
We're not scrap metal or "junk."
Just patriots, that can't be bought.
Just like the President, Donald J. Trump.

Ravens and Jaguars, what a mistake.
In 1776, God did "not" save the queen.
You took a knee for Britain's sake.
Please explain, what does that mean?
If schooled in civics, you "flunked."
Your own country, you forsake.
No king or queen here, just President Trump.

Jerome Dolenz

We don't pull the crowds, as you do. Most cowboys earn small pay. Maybe we will, when I get through. Fill our rodeo arenas, the American way. Dallas, your gesture really "stunk." Real cowboys ride with the red, white and blue. Not going to saddle up Trump.

No one is above the law.
At least we thought.
Our system is flawed.
From what we were taught.
Fake news is a dump.
Everyone should be in awe.
For the unfair treatment of Trump.

Scrutinize Washington D.C.
Where corruption all starts.
It trickles down, don't you see.
The "Left" is tearing us apart.
Players and Fans get "pumped."
Bring crooked Politicians to their knees.
We have the support of President Trump.

The Senate is a disgrace.
With the House in working order.
Everything else will fall into place.
Once we receive Senate supporters.
Senators get off your rumps.
Pass legislation, embrace.
Start supporting President Trump.

One has no Country.
Without a flag.
Taking a knee.
Is so, so sad.
Good Samaritan, NFL great Art Monk.
Mentoring kids, to succeed.
Taking the lead, is President Trump

Poetry with a Purpose

About the Author

Jerome "Jerry" Dolenz was born in Oklahoma and raised in western Kansas.

The third oldest sibling from a family of eleven. A veteran and married for thirty eight years.

He and his wife have been residents of Texas for twenty five years.

Poetry with a Purpose

www.ingramcontent.com/pod-product-compliance
Lightning Source LLC
Chambersburg PA
CBHW031427290426
44110CB00011B/553